HELP! MY CHILD IS BEING BULLIED

Tim Keeter

Consulting Editor: Dr. Paul Tautges

Help! My Child Is Being Bullied

ISBN
Paper: 978-1-63342-136-3
epub: 978-1-63342-137-0
Kindle: 978-1-63342-138-7

Published by **Shepherd Press**
P.O. Box 24
Wapwallopen, PA 18660

www.shepherdpress.com

All Scripture quotations, unless stated otherwise, are from the NASB.

Printed in Colombia

Designed by **documen**

Contents

INTRODUCTION

Parenting a child who is being bullied has many challenges. We notice all too well the ways in which our child is different from his or her peers: in physical stature (tall, short, underweight, overweight), socially, academically, artistic talent, lack of athletic skills, and so on. We treasure any moment when another child shows him or her kindness, and we pray earnestly, hoping for a genuine friend to emerge. At times, we can be hypersensitive to these differences, watching him or her interact with other children, analyzing every response, sideways glance, or snicker—hoping that, at the best, they keep their judgments to themselves.

Or perhaps your child typically doesn't have trouble fitting in and making friends, but something happens between him or her and a friend, one who is highly influential over the other boys or girls in the group. This friend, being displeased with your child, suddenly shows a dark and vengeful side.

And then it happens.

In those moments, our hearts are caught in a symphony of emotional dissonance: anger at the injustice, deep sorrow over the pain it causes our child, anxiety over how it will play out over time, regret over not having been able to prevent it, and perhaps even annoyance at having to deal with this at all ("Why can't my child just be more normal?").

Mom or Dad, I'm grateful you have picked up this mini-book. I want to encourage you right upfront that God's grace is sufficient for you; it's not on "pause." Instead, the Lord has provided parents with help and hope in his Word. In this mini-book, I will unpack biblical truths that, when applied to your heart, will put you in the best position to lead your child. I will guide you to discern how this trial opens the door to specific needs in your child's heart as well. Also, I will provide a plan for shepherding your child that is rich in God's promises, mercy, and hope.

I know from personal experience what it means to endure years of being bullied as a child, and I am aware of how it still affects me. As a child and teenager, I was very skinny and looked younger than my age. I weighed only 105 pounds when I graduated high school, and I didn't even look old enough to have a driver's license. My childhood occurred well before the digital age, so my altercations generally involved violence, public humiliation, or vandalism. Fast-forward a few decades, and I also know the pain of parenting a bullied child in the digital age, when bullies can do all the things I experienced as a child plus utilize social media to quickly expand their audience and sustain their attacks. When I was bullied it was hard and fearful at times, but to a child today, bullying can feel like a nonstop, merciless beating. Children who are bullied may feel they are helpless to defend themselves.

If you are a Christian parent, Jesus' death and resurrection means you do not have to sin in this trial. It means you are able to honor and obey your holy Father. It means you have access to the infinite wisdom of God. It means your sovereign Father will cause this trial to do you good. It means you have the God-given capacity to love those who sin against you and your family. It means you can boldly approach an understanding Savior to find deep compassion, the source of all comfort, and unfailing help in this time of need (Hebrews 4:15).

Please stop and pray right now for wisdom and grace to obey the Lord and persevere through this trial. And please keep reading.

1 What to Do First

When your child is being bullied there is great potential to allow your emotions to lead you away from acting with wisdom and self-control. Perhaps you've seen this to be true already. Or perhaps you are fighting against vengeful scenarios in your head that seem appealing but you know are not pleasing to God.

More information about what has happened and what will happen will likely come to light in God's purposeful timing. But how do you navigate the initial moments, when the outcome and details are still unknown?

You've probably heard the saying "Ready! Fire! Aim!" which pokes fun at those who tend to act before thinking. We need to be careful not to let that be characteristic of our response to bullying. Your "aim" is vital, and it is well worth the effort to consider where you are pointed before taking any further action. You need to know what the right destination is and how to get there. Where should the parent of a bullied child aim? I'll give you a hint: it's not at relief from the conflict.

Aim for God's Glory, Not Your Comfort

As parents, we want good things for our children. We want them to be liked and accepted by other children. We want them to be spared the pain of rejection and humiliation. We want them to be good friends and to have good friends. We want them to fit in, at least in the right ways. As a parent, you are to be commended for wanting these things.

But you cannot let those desires become so important to you that you pursue them at the cost of obedience to God or of being distracted from pursuing righteousness. The Bible informs us that when we do this, "good" things become idolatrous because they directly compete with Christ's rule in our hearts. If that becomes the case, your aim is tragically off the mark.

But does it really matter if you still get the issue resolved? Of course it matters, primarily because of what's at stake: God's glory. I don't want to trivialize the intensity and effect of this trial on your family, but this matter is way bigger than you or even your child.

> *Whether, then, you eat or drink or*
> *whatever you do, do all to the glory of God.*
> *(1 Corinthians 10:31)*

Here the apostle Paul reminds us that "whatever" we do, our aim is to bring glory and honor to God. This includes every aspect of your life, even parenting your child through the trial of bullying. Everything you do, think, or say has the potential to bring glory and honor to God, or to eclipse his grace and end up dishonoring him.

When the desire to glorify God is your aim, you can be confident that other desires will not be idolatrous. But when your desires for justice and relief overpower (become more important than) your desire for God's glory, then Jesus calls those desires "evil treasures":

> *The good man out of the good treasure of*
> *his heart brings forth what is good; and*
> *the evil man out of the evil treasure brings*
> *forth what is evil; for his mouth speaks*
> *from that which fills his heart.*
> *(Luke 6:45)*

It is critical for you to understand this truth: whatever governs your heart (your most powerful desire) is what governs your outward responses. Allow sinful treasures to rule, and sin comes out. But when the desire to honor God rules your heart, faithful obedience ensues. If you want God to be pleased with your response, you must first discern what you treasure the most.

In Luke 6:45, Jesus shows us how to discern what is reigning in our hearts: by observing the actions and attitudes that come out of us. At all times we leave a trail of evidence that exposes what's ruling our hearts. You can see this connection between inner treasures and outward responses in James:

> *For where jealousy and selfish ambition*
> *exist, there is disorder and every evil thing.*
> *But the wisdom from above is first pure,*
> *then peaceable, gentle, reasonable, full*
> *of mercy and good fruits, unwavering,*
> *without hypocrisy.*
>
> (James 3:16–17)

Make it your aim to bring glory and honor to God through faithful obedience in this trial. Like King David, ask the Lord to help you see what's ruling your heart:

Search me, O God, and know my heart;
Try me and know my anxious thoughts;
And see if there be any hurtful way in me,
And lead me in the everlasting way.
(Psalm 139:23–24)

If sinful treasures are exposed, confess them to God, rejoice in his forgiveness, and ask for his grace to turn from sin to faithful obedience.

Respond with Wisdom and Faith

How can you, as a Christian parent, initially respond to the realization that your child is being bullied? Here are six responses which will enable you to glorify God.

Discern the Urgency of the Situation

It is best to err on the side of caution regarding your child's physical safety. Ask specific questions about the threats, the individuals who are involved, and potential witnesses. Be sure to note any evidence of physical abuse. If there is any concern, first ensure your child's safety. Consult those in authority for advice and assistance so that the degree of action matches the potential threat, while you investigate the validity of the threat.

Reserve Judgment and Trust God

Not all threats are real, and no eyewitness is infallible, so it is wise to reserve judgment until you have gathered enough evidence to discern the situation. God's Word says it is foolish to respond hastily to something we have not yet sought to understand:

> *He who gives an answer before he hears,*
> *It is folly and shame to him.*
>
> (Proverbs 18:13)

It's also important to reserve judgment about God and why he is allowing this to happen. Regarding a different area of struggle (fighting depression), biblical counselor Bob Somerville encourages us to trust what we know about God when we don't understand the extent or outcome of our trials. This also applies to the trial of bullying.

> *I want to encourage you to suspend judgment for now and trust the One who does understand. Tell Him that even though you don't understand, you trust Him anyway and will let God be God. So what are you to do when it seems hopeless? It's helpful*

> *to recall what drew you to God in the first place—the hope He is able to offer you.*[1]

Solid hope is rooted in who God is, and it is nourished by his provisions for us, such as the Scriptures, the indwelling Holy Spirit, prayer, your church family, and wise counselors who have an exemplary love for Jesus and his Word.

Pray for and Seek Wisdom

God delights to give us wisdom when we need it. Therefore, James exhorts us to ask God for wisdom when we encounter various trials:

> *But if any of you lacks wisdom, let him ask of God, who gives to all generously and without reproach, and it will be given to him.*
>
> (James 1:5)

You also need wisdom because your child is watching and studying your response. Keep in mind the old parenting adage, "More is caught than is taught." You must model what you want your child to become in this trial. Do you want your child to trust God the way you are trusting him? To respond to being wronged the way you do? To pray as often as you pray? To find hope in the Scriptures to the same degree?

James goes on to say that when we ask for wisdom, we also need to trust God alone without being "double-minded." In other words, guard your thoughts and inner treasures from splitting your allegiance between the wisdom of God and the so-called wisdom of the world. Of course, we don't just pray for it and then sit around waiting for God to sprinkle "wisdom dust" on us and, poof! now we are wise! He gives wisdom through his Word, which means we need to regularly read, listen to, meditate upon, search, and receive the Word. As children of God, we have the indwelling Holy Spirit to help us understand and apply Scripture, as well as counsel from godly people in our lives (John 16:13–14; 1 John 2:20, 27; Proverbs 1:5).

Let these times of prayer be sweet between you and the Father. While you suffer, be honest about your confusion, hurt, and weaknesses. Honest prayer helps you to remember to place all your hope and dependence on Christ and his grace.

> *This hope we have as an anchor of the soul,*
> *a hope both sure and steadfast . . .*
>
> *(Hebrews 6:19)*

The "we" in this verse refers to believers in Jesus

Christ. But perhaps you or your child does not yet know Jesus Christ as your Lord and Savior. If that is the case, these promises are not accessible through willpower or self-discipline. The Bible teaches that we all are sinners by nature and by choice (Romans 3:23; Isaiah 53:6). We are weak and helpless, unable to save ourselves through religion, morality, or good works. So God came to our rescue. He showed his great love by sending his Son to be the one and only sacrifice for our sins (Romans 5:6–8). Jesus died for our sins, and he rose again the third day to show that his work to purchase our salvation is complete (Romans 4:25). God's solution to our spiritual problem is fully provided through the death and resurrection of Jesus on our behalf (2 Corinthians 5:21). By grace through faith in Jesus alone, we become a child of God, are indwelt by the Holy Spirit, and are progressively transformed into a new creation (2 Corinthians 5:17). In Christ, abundant hope and grace to endure any trial are now ours.

This is the gospel, the good news from God. Do you believe this message? If you have not yet turned to Jesus by faith, you may want to stop reading and spend some time in prayer. If you are already a Christian, you also may want to stop for a moment to pray for wisdom and grace to obey the

Lord and to persevere through this trial.

Gather Information, While Being Gracious and Humble

We saw above from Proverbs 18:13 that to avoid being foolish we need to "hear" a matter before we "answer" it. Neither you nor your child—nor any witness—is infallible or omniscient. You must continue to gather and weigh all the facts from as many perspectives as you can.

> The mind of the prudent acquires knowledge,
> And the ear of the wise seeks knowledge. . . .
> The first to plead his case seems right,
> Until another comes and examines him.
> (Proverbs 18:15, 17)

This means talking to potential witnesses and teachers. Make the appropriate teachers and authorities aware, asking how they can help and what they recommend you to do. When it's possible to talk with the parents of the suspected bully, be quick to listen, slow to speak, and even slower to anger:

> This you know, my beloved brethren. But everyone must be quick to hear, slow to speak and slow to anger; for the anger of

man does not achieve the righteousness of God.

(*James* 1:19–20)

Talking to your child may be difficult and even frustrating. Your child is not yet a mature adult, so you should expect him or her to make decisions and respond in ways that are unwise and even sinful. As you question and listen, keep in mind that there will be a time for patient instruction or even role-playing in order to prepare for future incidents. For now, however, focus on offering compassion, comfort, and correction that is gentle and humble. Your child is bruised and afraid. Like Jesus, be a friend of sinners who hurt. If your child has sinned through bitterness, sinful anger, seeking vengeance, or other sinful responses, guide him or her to confess to God and others, reminding your child that there is never an excuse for sinning against God, and that God is always faithful to forgive the repentant, over and over:

If we confess our sins, He is faithful and righteous to forgive us our sins and to cleanse us from all unrighteousness.

(1 *John* 1:9)

I personally find it helpful to remember that, even when we confront sin and must be firm in correction, we must speak with love and self-control:

> *But the fruit of the Spirit is love, joy, peace, patience, kindness, goodness, faithfulness, gentleness, self-control; against such things there is no law.*
>
> (Galatians 5:22–23)

Gathering information may also warrant printing or taking photos of online content ("cyberbullying") before the evidence is deleted or blocked from you. Do this as soon as possible.

An important question to answer early on is: "Is what happened/is happening actually bullying?" To help you discern the answer, consider a definition from the website stopbullying.gov:

> *Bullying is unwanted, aggressive behavior among school aged children that involves a real or perceived power imbalance. The behavior is repeated, or has the potential to be repeated, over time.*[2]

For something to be considered bullying, the following three characteristics must be concurrent:

1. An act or acts of an aggressive nature;
2. The presence of an imbalance of power (such as physical strength, access to embarrassing information, or popularity); and
3. Repetition.[3]

Acts of bullying can include threats, rumors, physical attacks, verbal attacks, and intentional exclusion from a group. Bullying can occur face-to-face or digitally (via social media, texting, email, online gaming sites, or other apps). Cyberbullying offers the opportunity for bullies to impose their tactics any time they desire. The anonymity and permanence of online material is also problematic.[4]

In general, it is wise for parents to be aware of their child's online activities. If cyberbullying occurs, you should consider reporting it to the school authorities and contacting any social media or gaming platforms being used. Most online platforms have policies in place in order to quickly discern and shut down the accounts of people who violate rules against cyberbullying.

In the case of a serious physical threat or criminal activity (including some cyber activities), you should report it to the police. God has put civil authorities in place to minister on his behalf as avengers of "the one who practices evil" (Romans 13:4). You are wise and within your rights to take advantage of protection offered by the civil government.

Be Angry, But Do Not Sin

As you gather information, and involve authorities as much as is needed, remember that the line between righteous parental anger and sinful anger can be very thin.

> *Be angry, and yet do not sin; do not let the sun go down on your anger, and do not give the devil an opportunity.*
>
> *(Ephesians 4:26–27)*

It is right to be angry when someone sins against your child in this manner. But righteous anger must remain under control. The divine anger revealed in the Bible is never the inner boiling, out-of-control response we know all too well from ourselves and others. Rather, it is a call to righteous action that is consistent with the fruit of the Spirit and appropriately addresses injustice.

We must recognize that we don't get to define injustice. God does. Rather, we weigh what we perceive has occurred against the question, "Would God agree that this is an injustice?" If the

Bible does not agree, our anger is likely selfishly motivated and thus cannot be righteous.

Provided you have sensed a true injustice, you should do something about it. You are not allowed to stuff anger down and let it boil, nor is it acceptable to blow up and misuse angry energy to attack others. So what are you to do? Pursue faithful obedience that honors God and points others to Christ. The particulars of your situation combined with governing principles in Scripture, wisely applied, dictate what that looks like. For example, confront the bully while exercising self-control and humility. Pray for the bully (Matthew 5:44). Or choose to let love cover the offense (1 Peter 4:8). In the book of Romans, Paul directs those who are being sinned against to always leave vengeance to the Lord and instead to pursue peace:

> *If possible, so far as it depends on you, be at peace with all men.*
>
> *(Romans 12:18)*

In doing this, you prepare yourself and your child to recognize that the other child and his or her parent(s) may never repent or display godly sorrow. Instead, make it your primary aim to bring glory and honor to God through faithful obedience, and trust him for everything else, including how other people respond.

Expect Only Good from God

One of my favorite Scripture passages is Romans 8:28–32. Let's consider it in two parts.

> *And we know that God causes all things to work together for good to those who love God, to those who are called according to His purpose. For those whom He foreknew, He also predestined to become conformed to the image of His Son, so that He would be the firstborn among many brethren; and these whom He predestined, He also called; and these whom He called, He also justified; and these whom He justified, He also glorified.*
>
> (Romans 8:28–30)

What is the "good" promised to believers in times of trial? The answer is given in verse 29: that God causes every trial to work toward the goal of conforming us "to the image of His Son." God uses every trial to make us more like Jesus. God employs every trial (including the bullying of your child) to do you good by helping you first to see specific needs for your own spiritual growth. In whatever ways you have fallen short of bringing glory to God in this trial, repent and take note of how you need to grow.

Is that promise "good" to you? It should be. We can desire no greater good than to be made more like our Redeemer and Great Shepherd. This is more important than "relief" from the trial. Faithful obedience in a trial forces you to do business with what's going on inside your heart—to nourish the "good treasures" and actively to forsake the "evil treasures."

Now let's consider the second part of the passage. Look at the amazing way it ends:

> *What then shall we say to these things? If God is for us, who is against us? He who did not spare His own Son, but delivered Him over for us all, how will He not also with Him freely give us all things?*
>
> (Romans 8:31–32)

We can stand on this promise because God has already met our greatest need by handing over his own Son to bear the wrath we justly deserve—so how could we ever doubt that he will give us anything else we really need?

2 A God-Honoring Response to Bullying

I hope the biblical principles in the last chapter encouraged you. Personally, I am all too aware of how often I fall short of God's best and have to fight off discouragement when my weaknesses and sin are exposed. But in the moments when you are tempted to be discouraged, look to Jesus and rely fully on God's abundant grace. Confess your sin, ask him to forgive you (believing that he does), and keep moving toward the disciplines of biblical thinking and faithful obedience. A pervasive love for God's wisdom and glory never fails to produce the fruit of faithful obedience.

As your situation develops, and you learn more and more details about the bullying, maintain your focus and recheck your aim: "Am I still pursuing the glory and honor of God above all things?" You probably cannot ask yourself that question too often.

Your answer should reflect your thoughts, attitudes, desires, and actions as they relate to this trial. That means how you think and act toward your family as well as other friends, witnesses, authorities, and even the bully. "Is the glory of God on my mind when I think about or talk about the bully?"

So what kinds of thoughts, attitudes, desires, and actions glorify God when your child is being bullied? Here are four qualities which can also be modeled and taught to your child.

Rest on God's Character

In any trial, great or small, my family has learned to lean heavily on a bit of timeless wisdom articulated by Jerry Bridges about the character of God:

> *We do not know the extent, the duration, or the frequency of the painful, adverse circumstances in which we must frequently trust God. We are always coping with the unknown. Yet it is just as important to trust God as it is to obey Him.*[5]

In addition, Bridges urges us to remember that at all times God is

1. Perfect in his love;
2. Infinite in his wisdom; and
3. Completely sovereign.[6]

There is so much to unpack in that short statement which is beyond the scope of this mini-book. So I encourage you to pursue a richer understanding of, and love for, the attributes of God throughout your life. The character of God matters, and as we grow to know and love his character more, it resonates in every aspect of our lives.

Be thankful that the God who reveals himself in the Bible is at all times perfect in his love, so he always *wants* what is best for you. Take comfort in a living, true God who not only wants what is best for you, but, in his infinite wisdom, also *knows* what is best for you . . . at all times. And you have a hope anchored in your great God who not only wants and knows what is best for you, but is all-powerful, so he will *never, ever fail* to bring about what he loves and desires.

What a relief that you don't have to know how it is all going to work out! Instead, you can trust God to accomplish his good and perfect will in everything, at all times. Your plan B is never even close to being better than God's plan. Scripture gives repeated testimony to our Father's benevolent, sovereign care:

> *Who is there who speaks and it comes to pass,*
> *Unless the Lord has commanded it?*

Is it not from the mouth of the Most High
That both good and ill go forth?
(Lamentations 3:37–38)

We know that God is never the direct cause of evil (James 1:13), but evil things that do not please God cannot occur unless he allows them (see, for example, the first two chapters of the Old Testament book of Job). That in no way absolves the bully of his or her responsibility—we all must directly answer for our sins. But it does help us understand that even though the bully is responsible for his or her actions, that bully does not have the authority or ability to ensure the *final outcome* of his or her actions. God alone determines these matters.

Praise God that the story doesn't end when bad things happen! If God allows a bully to sin against your child, then God has a loving, wise, and greater purpose that he will bring about as a result of that sinful action. Guaranteed! The fact that God brings good from evil only amplifies how excellent and wonderful he is!

» A pervasive love for God's wisdom and glory produces a faithful obedience that rests on God's character.

God has been faithful in the past and will continue to be faithful again. Therefore, match your concerns to deliberate reminders about God's character, just as one eighteenth-century hymnwriter wrote:

> *Be still, my soul; the Lord is on thy side;*
> *Bear patiently the cross of grief or pain;*
> *Leave to thy God to order and provide;*
> *In every change He faithful will remain.*
> *Be still, my soul; thy best, thy heavenly, Friend*
> *Through thorny ways leads to a joyful end.*[7]

Do the hard things that obedience demands, trusting that obeying God is always the best way forward and that it is never worth sinning against God.

> Cease striving and know that I am God;
> I will be exalted among the nations, I will be exalted in the earth.
>
> (Psalm 46:10)

Disciple Your Child

As parents, we have an important mission statement that is directly in line with the Great

Command given by Jesus to his bride, the church. Jesus charged the church with the task of making disciples in a fallen world:

> *Go therefore and make disciples of all the nations, baptizing them in the name of the Father and the Son and the Holy Spirit, teaching them to observe all that I commanded you; and lo, I am with you always, even to the end of the age.*
>
> (Matthew 28:19–20)

As Christian parents, we extend the church's obligation to make disciples into the domain of our homes. It is our privilege and duty to be busy about the task of shepherding our unbelieving children to salvation and then shepherding our believing children to grow in Christlikeness. We are always "on the job," not just when we are at church.

> *These words, which I am commanding you today, shall be on your heart. You shall teach them diligently to your sons and shall talk of them when you sit in your house and when you walk by the way and when you lie down and when you rise up.*
>
> (Deuteronomy 6:6–7)

As a parent, you are a full-time shepherd, a discipler. You disciple when you sit to eat with your child, do yardwork alongside him or her, prepare for school tests, involve your child in serving your church family, and even when you walk through your child's trial of being bullied. In fact, those moments of hurt and suffering in your child's life are rich soil within which discipleship can thrive. When your child has been bullied, his or her heart is exposed and in need of help; it is highly likely that you have your child's attention about spiritual things in a way you do not when life seems normal.

Do not waste this opportunity to point your child to Jesus. Even if you don't always know exactly what to say, you will never go wrong pointing him or her to the Great Shepherd. You can also take comfort that Christ is with you in your disciple-making (note how he finishes the Great Command with "I am with you always").

» A pervasive love for God's wisdom and glory produces a faithful obedience focused on shepherding your child toward gospel faith and faithfulness in a fallen world.

Address your child's concerns by reminding him or her that Jesus, having himself suffered, understands your child's suffering and offers him or her a real and lasting hope and comfort.

> *Therefore, since we have a great high priest who has passed through the heavens, Jesus the Son of God, let us hold fast our confession. For we do not have a high priest who cannot sympathize with our weaknesses, but One who has been tempted in all things as we are, yet without sin. Therefore let us draw near with confidence to the throne of grace, so that we may receive mercy and find grace to help in time of need.*
>
> (Hebrews 4:14–16)

Endure What Is Common to Mankind

There is hope in God's character, which is reflected in his loving, wise, and sovereign care for us in every trial. There is hope in Jesus, who has gone before us. He is sympathetic to us in our weaknesses, and freely offers mercy and grace in every trial. There is also strength in God's faithfulness and in our fellow brothers and sisters in Christ. Why? Because your present trial is a common one:

No temptation has overtaken you but such as is common to man; and God is faithful, who will not allow you to be tempted beyond what you are able, but with the temptation will provide the way of escape also, so that you will be able to endure it.
(1 Corinthians 10:13)

Sometimes it's easy to turn our thoughts inward and think we are all alone in our experience. But the apostle Paul strips that idea away from us. "No temptation" can be understood as "No trial" or "No trouble." While the particular combination of details in your trial may seem unique, Scripture asserts that the essence of your trial is *common*. That's comforting. Since your trial is common to man, you can be encouraged that many other believers have walked through similar trials in faithful obedience. So you can too! And you don't just share a common experience with those saints, but you also share a common Savior, who ensures you a decisive victory:

But in all these things we overwhelmingly conquer through Him who loved us.
(Romans 8:37)

Seek out brothers and sisters in your church family who have demonstrated wisdom and faithful obedience in their lives (even if they have not experienced bullying themselves). The church is a family given to us from God. Our brothers and sisters suffer with us, patiently comfort us, warn us when we need correction, and hold us up when we are weak (1 Thessalonians 5:14). By functioning as a faithful member of a church family, you teach your child the vital importance of the body of Christ in the life of every believer.

The rest of 1 Corinthians 10:13 points to two important outcomes of God's faithfulness.

First, God "will not allow you to be tempted beyond what you are able." Because God is faithful, he matches the sufficiency of his grace to the degree of your temptation or trouble, in order that you might endure. In Christ, you have all the grace you need to face and respond to this trouble with faithfulness. This also means that no matter how hard your trial gets, you never have an excuse to sin in response.

Second, God "will provide the way of escape also, so that you will be able to endure it." Because God is faithful, he always prepares a way out of your trials. It is important to note that this verse does not promise that the way out is a full resolution of the trouble or relief from the difficulty. It does promise an escape from anything that might overwhelm your ability to stand firm in your faith. God helps you to endure, or "bear up under" the load of the trial in faithful obedience. Your loving and wise Father sees you through to the end.

"How long must it go on?" Some trials can gradually wear down our will to fight. We become weak and weary, wondering if it will ever end, and we can even be tempted to despair. We don't know the answer to the "How long?" question, though we do know that the Bible calls even a lifelong trial "a little while" in comparison with our eternal glory:

> *After you have suffered for a little while,*
> *the God of all grace, who called you to His*
> *eternal glory in Christ, will Himself perfect,*
> *confirm, strengthen and establish you.*
> (1 Peter 5:10)

Not only does Peter here set the timeline of undesired events in our lives against the backdrop of eternity, but he also reminds us of God's purposes for his children in every trial: to be made more like Jesus. In Romans 8, Paul also speaks of suffering in light of eternity:

> *For I consider that the sufferings of this present time are not worthy to be compared with the glory that is to be revealed to us.*
>
> (Romans 8:18)

The glory bought for us by Jesus is so wonderful that even the worst sufferings of this world are not "worthy" to be compared with it.

» A pervasive love for God's wisdom and glory produces a faithful obedience that endures trials.

Continually redirect your family's gaze away from self and onto God's faithfulness and our eternal glory, given to us by grace, through faith, in Christ.

Overcome Evil with Good

The twelfth chapter of Romans begins with a command for our minds to be continually transformed so that we will live for Christ instead of conforming ourselves to worldly thinking and behavior. Shortly after that, and right on the heels of a command to love and practice hospitality to our brothers and sisters in the Lord, Paul gives us another very important command:

> *Bless those who persecute you; bless and do not curse. Rejoice with those who rejoice, and weep with those who weep.*
> (Romans 12:14–15)

This shift to "those who persecute you" is not disconnected from the previous thirteen verses. If we think and act like the unredeemed world, then we will curse those who wrong us and even seek to exact revenge. By contrast, if we are renewed in the Spirit (Romans 12:1–2), we will not only refrain from cursing and vengeance, but will actually seek to bless those who wrong us and will show genuine compassion toward them. You are to rejoice when things go well with them, rather than to return evil for evil by being envious. You are to weep compassionately with them when they experience hardship, rather than returning evil for evil by gloating.

God takes seriously how you respond to wrongs against you. Paul goes on in Romans 12 to categorically prohibit returning evil for evil or exacting revenge. "Vengeance is mine," declares the Lord. We simply do not have the right because we are not God. He alone is holy and perfect in his justice.

This command then follows:

Do not be overcome by evil, but overcome evil with good.

(Romans 12:21)

God not only prohibits returning evil for evil, but he also prohibits a stalemate! Indifference or ignoring the situation is not an option; rather, you are commanded to "overcome evil with good."

To be overcome by evil is to give in to worldly thinking, seeking to exact revenge and return evil for evil. Being overcome by evil means you allow evil treasures to rule your heart more than the love of Christ.[8] But to overcome evil with good means you continue to be faithfully obedient even in the face of personal injury. It means you live in a Christ-honoring way toward everyone, including your enemies, showing humility (Romans 12:3, 16), helpfulness (12:6–8), and peacefulness to all (12:18). You and your child need to intentionally and purposefully bless those who have wronged (and even continue to wrong) you, to show them kindness, and to pray for God to do good in their lives.[9]

I realize how hard this may seem right now. That's why we don't look to ourselves to obey these good commands. We rely on the love of Christ within us to live for the glory and honor of Christ:

For the love of Christ controls us, having concluded this, that one died for all, therefore all died; and He died for all, so that they who live might no longer live for themselves, but for Him who died and rose again on their behalf.

(2 Corinthians 5:14–15)

» A pervasive love for God's wisdom and glory produces a faithful obedience that purposely seeks to return good for evil.

Pray regularly for the bully—for God to bless him or her. Ask God to help you forsake anything within you that promotes sinful, vengeful attitudes and responses. Ask Jesus to help you and your child plan to show kindness to the bully when given an opportunity. Aren't you grateful that God did this and more for you?

But God demonstrates His own love toward us, in that while we were yet sinners, Christ died for us.

(Romans 5:8)

In summary, you will be prepared to shepherd the heart of your child when you intentionally cultivate a pervasive love for God's wisdom and glory. Apply God's wisdom in faithful obedience that

1. Rests on God's character;
2. Is focused on shepherding your child toward gospel faith and faithfulness in a fallen world;
3. Endures trials with gospel-centered hope; and
4. Purposely seeks to return good for evil.

We are now ready to focus in on the parenting task between you and your child—the heart work that the Lord has lovingly placed in your hands through this trial of bullying. You will be more effective at imparting God-honoring wisdom and hope to your child when you are pursuing it yourself. It's as if you are saying to your child, "Follow me, as I follow Christ."

3 The Heart of Your Bullied Child

Your bullied child needs specific parental counsel. Therefore, you need to understand what is going on in his or her heart. This chapter summarizes four categories of sinful ways children typically respond to being bullied. You can use these broad categories to ask specific questions of your child and learn what combination of these may be driving his or her interpretations and responses. Chapter 4 provides biblical application to help you and your child address these issues.

When the Bible speaks of the heart, it addresses what we may summarize as "the inner man." In Scripture, the heart is always active. It thinks, reasons, and desires. It also has treasures, affections, a will, emotions, a conscience, attitudes, and motives. A very important aspect of the heart always to keep in mind is that it is tightly linked to behavior, as illustrated in the diagram.

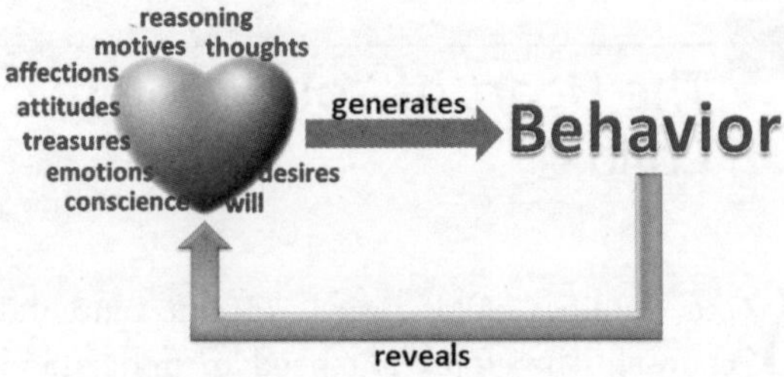

The Bible teaches that what's going on in your heart determines your behavior, and the same is true of your child. The good news is that by careful observation of your child's behavior, you can discern what is going on in his or her heart. Understanding this important dynamic has made a world of difference in my life as a believer and has impacted my marriage and parenting.

Two Buckets

For starters, we can separate behavior into two buckets: sinful and obedient. In Chapter 1 we saw from Luke 6:45 that sinful behavior is produced by sinful "treasures" in our hearts. Conversely, faithful obedience is produced by treasures in our hearts that are consistent with godliness. Why is this important? Because if you want to parent your child so that his or her heart "brings forth what is good," you need to

1. Understand the sinful treasures residing in your child's heart that are generating sinful responses;
2. Show your child the way of repentance;
3. Teach your child about the good treasures that should replace the sinful ones; and
4. Help your child pray for and cultivate good treasures that will bring forth God-honoring obedience.

By helping our children make the connection between their behavior and the treasures in their hearts, we can enable them to develop an awareness of what really makes them tick.

However, plumbing the depths of your child's heart is not always easy. Be patient and gentle in the process. It often takes many conversations addressing different situations over time to gain enough context to confidently discern a child's heart. A good way to help you gain insight into your child's heart is to ask questions about a specific situation or event, such as:

» "What is important to you right now?" "What do you want to happen?" (to reveal sinful treasures and desires).

» "What *should* be important to you right now?" (to direct your child to godly treasures that need to replace the sinful ones).

I hope you can see why this line of questioning is more effective than "Why did you do that?" or "What should you do next time?" Your child has no hope of lasting, God-honoring change without the indwelling Holy Spirit and will still miss the mark if change doesn't zero in on the heart as the source of his or her behavior.

Four Problematic Responses

Here are four categories to explore that are common problems among bullied children. This list is not exhaustive, but it should help you form an agenda right away.

Escaping Unwanted Emotions

As we learned in Chapter 1, we can easily slip into wanting something so much that it becomes an idolatrous desire. For the bullied child (and for us!), it can be tempting to focus on wanting to be free from intense, painful emotions to the degree that it becomes a sinful treasure that generates sinful behavior. A sinful treasure in Luke 6:45 can be something that is clearly sinful (like selfish ambition) or just something that is OK to want in principle (like wanting to get past the horrible feeling of humiliation) but has evolved from an inward desire to a demand.

Here are some outward behaviors that may be evidence of such a demand within your child's heart:

- He avoids talking about the bullying, even to the point of withdrawal or deception. The reason for avoidance in this case is primarily because talking about it brings up the unwanted emotions he is actively trying to suppress: "I don't want to talk about it because it makes me feel awful!"
- She controls or suppresses her feelings in unbiblical ways. This sometimes looks like finding refuge in other things like hobbies, food, forms of entertainment, cutting, alcohol, or drugs.
- He becomes hopeless, as if he doesn't see a way out that will bring the relief he strongly desires.
- She uses various expressions reflecting the idea that "I would be truly happy if I could avoid feeling this way."

Negative Self-Perception

Sadly, bullies often capitalize on differences between your child and others. This is an obvious snare that can tempt your child to buy into these comparisons. Listen for these kinds of comparisons and ask specific questions about what your child believes is different about him- or herself, whether or not the differences are good or bad, and what difference your child thinks it would make if he or she was more like others. In this line of questioning, you are trying first to understand your child's own perceptions of him- or herself, the values that are reflected in your child's self-perceptions, and how your child is responding.

Bitter Spirit

Your bullied child has been wronged, but in hurt and humiliation is he or she responding with a bitter spirit and unwilling to "overcome evil with good" (see Chapter 2)? Here are some possible signs to look for:

» Bitterness or anger toward the bully, those who joined in with the bully, or even a teacher for not protecting him or her;

- » Replaying the event(s) over and over in his or her mind;
- » Entertaining fantasies about, or plots for, revenge;
- » Deriving pleasure from imagining bad things happening to the bully;
- » Making statements like, "I wish I could get [the bully] back!"; or
- » Demonstrating prideful responses like, "Why does everyone think I'm stupid? I'm smarter than all of those idiots!" (This was my personal go-to as a bullied child.)

Fear of Man

God's Word warns us about developing an over-anxious concern about what others think, primarily because it erodes our trust in the Lord. The Bible refers to this preoccupation with other people as the "fear of man":

> *The fear of man brings a snare,*
> *But he who trusts in the* Lord *will be exalted.*
> *(Proverbs 29:25)*

This is a common and powerful temptation for many bullied children, but we must help them see the truth about this deceptive trap. It is actually a form of pride and self-centeredness. In part, it exalts the opinions of other people above God's. It deceives children into believing they need other people to gratify, serve, or respect them in order to be happy. It takes their eyes off Jesus and fixes them on themselves as the center of their world, rather than God.

> *For am I now seeking the favor of men, or of God? Or am I striving to please men? If I were still trying to please men, I would not be a bond-servant of Christ.*
>
> *(Galatians 1:10)*

Understanding the specifics about what is going on in the heart of your child is an important step, but it is not the last step. God meets our troubles with solutions, and there is no idolatry that is too great or too entrenched in your child's heart for God's truth and grace. No matter what your present situation is, there is hope and help for your child right now.

4 Hope and Help for Your Bullied Child

The principles explained so far, which you model and pass along to your child, will go a long way toward pointing your child to Jesus. There is simply nothing more important you can do for your child in this or any other trial. Through Jesus Christ, God brought the greatest good ever out of the worst suffering ever, and it should be a tremendous comfort and hope that Jesus knows your child's suffering and yours as well. There is hope and help in your Great Shepherd.

There is also hope and help in repentance. If you or your child sins during the trial, do not delay repentance. In the Bible, true repentance is more than just making a verbal confession; it always involves a turning from sin and toward righteousness as well as the bearing of fruit as evidence of that turning.

Now let's take each of the four problematic responses mentioned in Chapter 3 and shine the light of Scripture on them.

Move from Escaping Unwanted Emotions toward Patient Hope in God

God doesn't want us to avoid talking about our pain. He encourages us to do so. Teach your child honestly to express what he or she is feeling to God who cares, just as Asaph in Psalm 73 and so many other psalmists prayed:

> *When I pondered to understand this,*
> *It was troublesome in my sight.*
>
> *(Psalm 73:16)*

Our expressions should always avoid sinful anger or charging God with fault. Instead, help your child to cry out to God, to admit his or her weakness and doubts, and to ask God for help to rest in and expect God's continuing faithfulness.

Similarly, God doesn't want us to resort to sinful means of escape from a trial. Instead, it pleases him for us to bear up under the load while relying on his grace, his timing, and his promises in the trial. Go back and review the section "Endure What Is Common to Mankind" in Chapter 2. Note from Peter's first letter that Christ's example was not to return insults or threats, but to trust God instead:

> *For you have been called for this purpose, since Christ also suffered for you, leaving you an example for you to follow in His steps, who committed no sin, nor was any deceit found in His mouth; and while being reviled, He did not revile in return; while suffering, He uttered no threats, but kept entrusting Himself to Him who judges righteously.*
>
> (1 Peter 2:21–23)

Move from Negative Self-Perception toward an Accurate View of Self

My favorite tool for helping people think through self-perceptions is one I picked up during my counselor training (see diagram). You can sketch this out on a piece of paper or a whiteboard, for example, and go through it with your child.

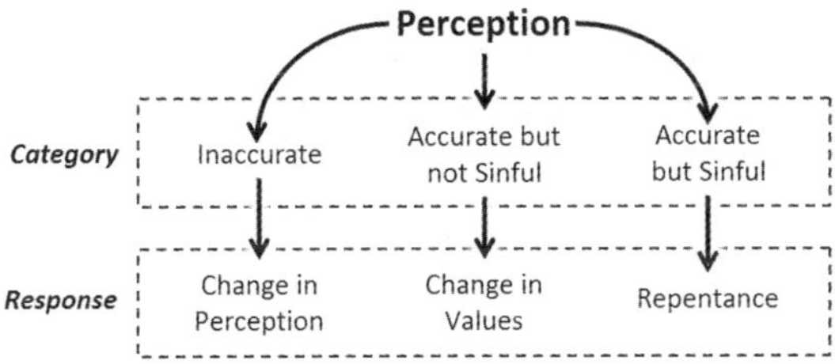

The idea is to take each perception and first categorize it as inaccurate, accurate but not sinful, or accurate and sinful. The biblical response then follows from each categorization. Inaccurate perceptions (e.g., "I *always* mess *everything* up") need to be changed to perceptions that are true or accurate. Accurate perceptions that are not sinful may require a change in what your child values as important (e.g., "I am not good at sports"). Accurate perceptions that are sinful require biblical repentance (e.g., "I have a bad temper").

For example, "I am skinnier and smaller than all the other boys" may be accurate, but it is not sinful. It reflects the way a holy, wise, and loving God made him. It is not a comparison that bears weight with the Lord, so it should not bear weight with us, even if others draw attention to it. Instead, God values love for him and for other people (Matthew 22:37–39). Going through this exercise is not an instantaneous fix. It will take time as your child regularly prays, memorizes Scripture, thinks, and recalls biblical truth whenever tempted to think poorly of his stature.

Move from a Bitter Spirit toward Compassionate Kindness

> *So, as those who have been chosen of God, holy and beloved, put on a heart of compassion, kindness, humility, gentleness and patience; bearing with one another, and forgiving each other, whoever has a complaint against anyone; just as the Lord forgave you, so also should you.*
>
> (Colossians 3:12–13)

It shouldn't take much reflection on the gospel to put circumstances into perspective when others wrong us. Why not? Because we have wronged God infinitely more. Granted, moving from bitterness toward what Paul exhorts in Colossians 3:12–13 will cost you and your child—not in cash dollars, but in the currency of humility, patience, and trust in the God who owns exclusive rights to ultimate justice. But you can be sure it will never cost you more than what it cost God to forgive you.

This may be a good time to review the section "Overcome Evil with Good" in Chapter 2.

With your child, ask the Lord to help both of you to grow in kindness and compassion toward the bully. Express concern for the bully's relationship with God, since by doing you harm the bully is in rebellion against a holy God, a terrible position to be in for sure! Then work on replacing hurtful thoughts with thoughts consistent with what we read in Philippians 4:8; specifically, thoughts that are

» Right: thinking from God's point of view;
» Admirable: reflecting on the good in the other person as opposed to faultfinding;
» Lovely: considering how you can serve or build up others (including the bully).[10]

Move from Fear of Man toward Fear of God

As discussed in Chapter 3, fear of man is a sin that must be confessed to the Lord. The solution, however, does not stop there. Help your child see the need to turn from his or her tendency to be overly concerned about what others think of him or her, and to turn toward cultivating a greater concern about what God thinks, and a reverent awe of God. The Bible calls this the "fear of God."

The most important resource for growing in the fear of God is, of course, the Bible, and you and your child cannot read, study, memorize, meditate upon, and talk about it enough. Prayer in response to the Bible will further help generate a fear of God and an awareness of his presence.

There are a number of helpful resources about the fear of God, and how to cultivate it, in the "Where Can I Get More Help?" section at the end of this mini-book. You may also want to ask your pastor for his recommendations.

Conclusion

At the beginning of this mini-book, I asked you to keep reading. I want to thank you for doing that. I hope and trust the biblical counsel provided will help your family to honor God while you walk through the trial of bullying.

Where are you and your child headed from here? Perhaps you are headed for more pain and humiliation, more nights of gut-aching sorrow, more tears, more sinful responses from which to repent, and more unresolved injustices. I pray that is not the case, but, if it is, you can be confident and take comfort in knowing that your loving, wise, sovereign Father and Savior will be faithful through it all.

Take refuge in the Father of mercies and the God of all comfort. He will never, ever, leave you, nor forsake you (Hebrews 13:5). No bully can change that! Apply the biblical counsel provided in this mini-book. Persevere, with your eyes fixed on eternity, knowing that one day, when sin has been conquered and put away once and for all, we will sing his praises with a sea of worshippers, "Great is Thy Faithfulness!"

Personal Application Projects

Throughout this mini-book, I have included practical application and exercises to help you shepherd your children in the ways of the Lord. In addition, here are a few application projects.

1. Create "Think Lists"

The way you and your child interpret, reason, and think through this issue is key to your spiritual growth. A good method to practice your thinking is to make short lists that include Scripture and brief, summary statements. Then regularly review, memorize, and pray through the list until it becomes more natural in your thinking. I recommend going back through this mini-book to identify sentences and passages you found helpful. For example,

> *"Even if I cannot see a way out of this trial,*
> *I can trust God to always be faithful—*
> *1 Corinthians 10:13."*

2. Do Acts of Service

Regularly serving others, especially those in your church family, is an important part of being a believer. Listen to others who are suffering in your church family. Help your child to develop compassion for them, and plan ways (with your child) to encourage them. For example, have your child send a card to share something that he or she is learning, and look for ways to meet physical needs (meals, yard work, housework, etc.).

3. Bless the Bully

Pray daily for the bully. Ask God to help you grow in kindness and compassion toward him or her and ask God to bless him or her. If you have a picture of your child with the bully (perhaps back when they were friends), put it on your child's desk to help him or her remember to pray.

Plan tangible ways to return good for evil; for example, a deliberate act of kindness, showing preference, speaking kindly to or about him or her. Keep track as your child accomplishes them.

Where Can I Get More Help?

Books

Adams, Jay E., *How to Overcome Evil* (Phillipsburg, NJ: Presbyterian & Reformed, 1977).

Priolo, Lou, *The Heart of Anger: Practical Help for Prevention and Cure of Anger in Children* (Amityville, NY: Calvary Press, 1997).

Sande, Ken, *The Peacemaker: A Biblical Guide to Resolving Personal Conflict* (Grand Rapids: Baker, 1990).

Tautges, Paul, *Raising Kids in a "You Can Do It!" World* (Leyland: 10Publishing, 2018).

Tripp, Tedd, *Shepherding a Child's Heart* (Wapwallopen, PA: Shepherd Press, 2005).

Tripp, Tedd, and Margie, *Instructing a Child's Heart* (Wapwallopen, PA: Shepherd Press, 2008).

Welch, Edward T., *When People Are Big and God Is Small: Overcoming Peer Pressure, Codependency, and the Fear of Man* (Phillipsburg, NJ: Presbyterian & Reformed, 1997).

Online or Other Resources

- Visit Institute for Biblical Counseling and Discipleship at www.ibcd.org for audio recordings of Ken Sande and general topics like parenting, peacemaking, and dealing with conflict.
- Visit Biblicalcounseling.org for general topics like parenting, peacemaking, and dealing with conflict.

The following resources can help you better understand the various forms of bullying, protective actions you can take, and common responses of bullied children, from a secular perspective:

- The US government website stopbullying.gov.
- The *Be Strong: Stop Bullying* app.

Endnotes

1 Bob Somerville, *If I'm a Christian, Why Am I Depressed?* (self-pub., Xulon Press, 2014), 34.

2 "What Is Bullying," www.stopbullying.gov/what-is-bullying/index.html.

3 Ibid.

4 Ibid.; and "What Is Cyberbullying," https://www.stopbullying.gov/cyberbullying/what-is-it/index.html.

5 Jerry Bridges, *Trusting God Even When Life Hurts* (Colorado Springs, CO: NavPress, 1994), 17–18.

6 Adapted from Bridges, *Trusting God Even When Life Hurts*, 18.

7 Katharina von Schlegel, "Be Still, My Soul," translated by Jane Borthwick.

8 William Hendriksen and Simon J. Kistemaker, *Exposition of Paul's Epistle to the Romans*, vol. 12–13, New Testament Commentary (Grand Rapids: Baker, 1953–2001), 423.

9 Ibid.

10 For an excellent treatment of how to apply Philippians 4:8, I highly recommend John Vandegriff, *In the Arena of the Mind* (Howell, NJ: Ask, Seek, and Knock, 1992).

Books in the Help! series include...

Help! Disability Pressures Our Marriage
Help! He's Struggling with Pornography
Help! I Can't Forgive
Help! I Can't Get Motivated
Help! I Can't Handle All These Trials
Help! I Feel Ashamed
Help! I Have Breast Cancer
Help! I Need a Church
Help! I Want to Change
Help! I Want to Model Submission in Marriage
Help! I'm a Single Mom
Help! I'm a Slave to Food
Help! I'm Anxious
Help! I'm Being Deployed
Help! I'm Confused About Dating
Help! I'm Depressed
Help! I'm Drowning in Debt
Help! I'm In a Conflict
Help! I'm In A Painful Marriage
Help! I'm Living With Terminal Illness
Help! I'm So Lonely
Help! I've Been Traumatized by Combat
Help! My Anger is Out of Control
Help! My Friend is Suicidal
Help! My Grandchild Has A Disability
Help! My Kids Are Viewing Pornography
Help! My Parents Abused Me When I Was A Kid
Help! My Spouse Has Been Unfaithful
Help! My Teen is Rebellious
Help! My Teen Struggles With Same-Sex Attractions
Help! My Toddler Rules the House
Help! She's Struggling With Pornography
Help! Someone I Love Has Alzheimer's
Help! Someone I Love Has Been Abused
Help! Someone I Love Has Cancer

More titles in preparation

For current listing go to:
https://www.shepherdpress.com/store/lifeline/

About Shepherd Press Publications

» They are gospel driven.

» They are heart focused.

» They are life changing.

Our Invitation to You

We passionately believe that what we are publishing can be of benefit to you, your family, your friends, and your work colleagues. So we are inviting you to join our online mailing list so that we may reach out to you with news about our latest and forthcoming publications, and with special offers.

Visit:

www.shepherdpress.com/newsletter

and provide your name and email address.